— I WAS —
BORN
—TO—
DEW

ANDREW (DEW) HENSON

authorHOUSE®

AuthorHouse™
1663 Liberty Drive
Bloomington, IN 47403
www.authorhouse.com
Phone: 1 (800) 839-8640

Published by AuthorHouse 10/06/2017

ISBN: 978-1-5462-0738-2 (sc)
ISBN: 978-1-5462-0737-5 (e)

Print information available on the last page.

Any people depicted in stock imagery provided by Thinkstock are models,
and such images are being used for illustrative purposes only.
Certain stock imagery © Thinkstock.

This book is printed on acid-free paper.

Because of the dynamic nature of the Internet, any web addresses or links contained in
this book may have changed since publication and may no longer be valid. The views
expressed in this work are solely those of the author and do not necessarily reflect the
views of the publisher, and the publisher hereby disclaims any responsibility for them.

Contents

"I would like to encourage you to use the blank pages throughout this book to create your own work of art, whether it be a poem, or a picture."

Struggle

Obstacles come obstacles go
Triumphant I am, this I know
Fear, a path in my way
Pain, the price I have to pay
Drive, my ability to keep pushing
Patience, the force to prevent rushing
Awareness, my vision to see all
Durability, my power to handle the toughest fall
Size, a defect that holds me back
Leadership, a trait I never lack
Pride, emotions I express
100%, show plenty more but nothing less
Captain, I put my teammate first
When I hear the gun, I sprint in in a really quick burst
Injuries may halt my performance
Stressing my body, enhancing my endurance
I am who I am and I do what I do
Call me what you want but I go by Dew
My young life has not always been true
There are many obstacles I power through
I am bothered by many things but I won't let that be you

Because Of You

When I need you the most you are there
When I am down you are there
When I am in trouble you are there
When I don't think I can do it you tell me I can
When I need anything you provide for me
When I do something good you reward me
When I was making bad decisions you were there
When I was about to be taken you begged
When I promised to change you said "I love you"
When I tried out for track you were proud
When I got my first medal you treasured it
When I got all academic honors you hugged me
When I got my first college letter you cried with me
When I graduate high school you will be there
When you leave for a better place I will be there
You are the world to me
Mom I love you with all of my heart
Everything I do, I do because of you

Careful What You Wish For

People often wish their dreams would come true
I wish I was a billionaire
I wish I was accepted
I wish I was immortal
I wish I was popular
I wish I was a genius
I wish I had friends
I wish my parents were always there
But people remain unaware of dreams
A nightmare is also a dream
And a nightmare and a dream can both become a reality
Careful what you wish for

It All Starts With You

My name
I didn't have one until you named me
My form
I didn't have one until you shaped me
My knowledge
I didn't have any until you taught me
My dreams
I didn't have any until you inspired me
My goals
I didn't have any until you set the bar
My existence
I wasn't here until you created me
You have creativity
I am your creation
I am an original
And I am unique

Emotions

What are emotions?
Emotions are feelings that you express
Joy
Anger
Pain
Nervousness
Sadness
Being overwhelmed
But how do you express them?
Different people have different ways
Such as actions
Such as languages
Or even facial expression
But they can all be misleading
So for example
Don't assume someone is sad because they are crying
Or that someone is mad because they are screaming
So express yourself
Emotions shape your character

Everything Happens For A Reason

Doors are open
Some close when their purpose has been fulfilled
Some remain open because it is the destined path
The past is what shapes you're present and future
The past struggles and triumphs are what shapes you
Death, loss of love, finding love, achieving your goals
There are so many life altering events that can make a person
The best way is often times frowned upon
Let the past die and embrace your experiences
For they can make or break the present
Never give up on your dreams, for giving up is losing
And you never win a race when you never see to the end
And always trust your gut
It can lead you to the wrong road
Or it can lead you to the right one
No matter what road you walk on, it may never be a smooth ride
Hope is an essential part with your heart
Good will come when it is time
But darkness will forever remain
It takes darkness for a star to shine
That is why bad things happen to good people
and good things happen to bad people
It all happens for a reason

Fear

My biggest fear
Not of spiders
Not of snakes
Not of heights
Not of Dying
But that I am powerful
Powerful beyond measure
Stuck up in my own ability
And failing to acknowledge others
Others who may need my guidance
For I want to influence others
Influence them to be better
To gain Confidence
And lift and inspire those around them

February

Granted it will forever be the shortest month of the year
It is still a great month
Not only is it the month I was born
It is the only month affected in a leap year
It is the month of love
But most importantly it is the month to
celebrate African Americans
This is the month they are honored for paving the way in society
Chuck Cooper
The first African American to be drafter to the NBA
Doug Williams
The first African American to lead his team to a super bowl win
Jackie Robinson
The first African American to play major league baseball
The 1966 Texas Western basketball team
The first team to win the NCAA Championship
with five African American starters
Olympic medalists Tommie Smith and John Carlos
Held up their fists during their medal
ceremony in support of black power
Rosa Parks
Had the courage to tell a white man NO!
Martin Luther King Jr.
Never gave up on his dream
Barack Obama
The first African American president
There are so many others who have contributed

The great thing, they were not all African American
They all came together in hopes for equality
There were so many people treated poorly
But it has proven to be for a good cause
Just look around the world
Look at all the African Americans that make a difference
And you will see why February is an important month of the year

Fight

Forcing yourself
Into never
Giving up
Hope for
The prize

Forever I Am Here

It started as an option
It turned to a passion
I used to call you nerds
I now call you family
Scream at you I must
Cleanse you of all your rust
Seven names to call me captain
So much to me it means
From a thug to a runner
A choice will never regret
No matter how hard it may seem
This all came as if it were a dream
Friends I gain for life
I have a message to you all
Three years I have been here
Never easy it has been
Although my term has come to an end
You will thrive as a force
I love you all as brothers and sisters
I am here if ever the need
Miss you I will, forget you I won't

Forgiveness

Forgiving people is a beautiful thing
Everyone commits to uneducated actions
But is forgiveness the right action
I have bullied someone
I have jumped someone
I have brutally beaten someone
In the end I was always forgiven
We are yet to become friends
We rarely ever talk
We never hang out
But we get along to sit in the same class
It amazes me on how heartless I was
But impresses me on other peoples will to forgive
An amazing writer
A pretty good singer
A really funny kid
All felt my wrath of terror
Granite I don't necessarily regret or feel bad of my actions
I will acknowledge that I was the one that was wrong
Whether it be harsh words
Or to fit in with a bad group of people
To the people that I have done wrong and forgave me
You have all my thanks and apologies

Greatness

What does it mean to be great?
What is considered to be a great thing?
What do you have to do in order to be considered to be great?
Being great is hard to explain
Something that everyone accepts and embraces can be great
Something that everyone frowns upon can be great
World-War one and two were great events
Bloodshed, families ruined, and so much money wasted
I hear about the casualties, and the
conditions and it makes me cry
Although they were tragic events, they were also great events
The passing of the 19th amendment
Woman finally earned their right to vote
Martin Luther King Junior was a great man
Very easily one of the greatest men to ever live
He was such a powerful man, using powerful wards and wisdom
Harriette Thompson and Fauja Singh both
achieved a great accomplishment
Harriette Thompson was the oldest female
marathon finisher at 92 years old
Fauja Singh was the oldest male marathon
finisher at an insane 101 years old
I achieve great things every single day
Great things don't have to be well known
I achieved greatness when I decided to change my lifestyle
Ordinary people do great things and
great people do ordinary things

Big towns raise nobodies and small towns raise somebodies
Nobodies and grow in to somebodies and
somebodies and grow into nobodies
No matter who you are and where you're from
You can be great

Growing Up

When your little you have many dreams
Not knowing how hard they are to accomplish
Maybe you need school
Maybe you have a defect
Maybe you don't have the motivation
Maybe you grew up in a bad place
But when it comes down to it
Dreams depend on you
They don't come true
They are made true

I Am A Fighter

I don't like being told no
I don't like conserving my abilities
I don't wish I was anyone outside of myself
I fight to obtain my name
I strive because it is essential
I work to assure that I am entertained
I scream to express myself
I cry to show my emotion
That's just me
And me is forever who I will be
When I look in the mirror me is the person that I see
And the view may not be very glamorous
But I don't care
Because my features attract very little glare
But my abilities will force you to stare
A life style can alter one's mindset
Because not everyone gets the opportunity to sleep in a bed
But the economy is not necessarily the reason for what I just said
Knowing that in order to make it, you need to use your head
Considering that not everyone gets the
concept of a pencil with lead
A disorder is no reason that we should not be fed
Because in the end everyone's blood turns from blue to red
And eventually everybody will turn up to be dead

I Let You Get Away

My heart hurts so much
My chest is filled with so much pain
Life without you can never be the same
You can't be one to take the blame
Because I was the one who did wrong
And now it is officially over
I am so lost in my life
We started as friends
And I denied my feelings
You wanted more
And I did too, but I was scared
You always tried to be there but I always left
I thought you were too good for me
The best person I ever met
But I finally found the courage
And I looked you in the eyes
Such a beautiful soul you had
I tried to mend what I tore
But the damage was too fatal
And my return was too late
You found someone else
I can't ever forget your smile
But I will always regret my choices
And your presence in my life will be deeply missed

I Run

I run because it's fun
As good as I get someone is always better
As hard as I try someone is always faster
When I try I usually die
When it's over I sometimes cry
Because I know I gave it my all
Knowing I would have finished even if I had to crawl
There is no denying my skill
Considering they come all without pills
I practice as hard as I can
From the first time I ever ran
And that is what has turned me into a man

I Will Forever Love You

I lost you a few years back
And it breaks my heart to know that I let
you slip through the cracks
How do I revive my broken heart
When the agony of losing you is tearing me apart
My mind is consumed by memories of you
Your soul is the prettiest that I ever knew
How do I look forward to a brand new day
With the only one that I ever loved having gone away
I see the beautiful sparkling eyes that lay upon your face
I see your perfect smile that fills my heart with grace
My dreams are filled with memories of our very first kiss
When I wake up I mourn over all that I miss
It seems that I am always in need of assistance
But our reunion is approaching in the distance
You were my very first love
And you flew away like a graceful little dove
I loved you enough to make you my wife
And I will continue to love you, even if you are not a part of my life

If I Knew

If I knew right from wrong
If I knew good from bad
If I knew false from true
If I knew the result of my decisions
If I knew how to respect adults
If I knew how to interact with my peers
If I knew how to control my anger
If I knew my future
If I knew the terror I would cause
If I knew the relationships I would abuse
I would not be me

Now That

Now that I know my past
Now that I know my mistakes
Now that I know my destruction
It makes me respect my actions
I am honored to have had the childhood that I did
Although it may not have been pleasant
I can relate to allot of people
My actions and have shaped who I am
Regret is an absent state in my mind
Now that I know who I am

I'm Not But I Am

Flawless I am not
Immortal I am not
Perfect I am not
Determined I am
Determined to change
Determined to learn
Determined to improve
Determined to win
Determined to make a difference
Determined to influence others
I may not be flawless
I may not be immortal
I may not be perfect
But I am determined

It's The Inside That Matters

I approached the mansion
Only to see that it was abounded and run down
I was at risk of retreat
But I saw a butterfly in the distance
It looked dreadful from afar
But I proceeded to disease our distance
As I drew nearer, I saw this vivacious garden
It was consumed by impeccable beauty
As I made my escapade through the breathtaking array
The aroma and the color smacked me in the face
As my expedition descended deeper
I locked eyes on a jaw dropping figure
It looked as if a statue made of marble
As I approached it, I began to realize
The view began to change
All I saw was you

Just A Kid

So many kids around the world
Some fall short the opportunity at adult hood
Some grow to be prison birds
Some grow to be successful adults
Whether you pass by the hand of SIDS
Or you die of a drug overdose
You may be convicted of rape
But you may grow to be a professional athlete
Or even the president of the United Sates
Whatever you grow to be in your life
You will forever be but one thing
You are just a plain ordinary kid from somewhere

Just Believe

He shows me how mighty he is
When he made me it was a message
A message to prove his greatness
I almost died at birth
I am about to turn 19
I am asthmatic
I run track and cross country
I am epileptic
I am forbidden to attend many parties
I have a short temper
I get mad over silly things
I had a terrible childhood
I am wiser than the average person my age
I am really goofy
I do silly stuff because that is just me
The good Lord has proven his greatness
He has showed it through me
That with all the setbacks in an individual's life
That individual can still succeed
They just have to believe

Live A Life That Matters

What is the purpose of life?
It is to fulfill a deed that matters
It does not matter on the luxuries that you buy
But on the kingdom that you build
Not the goods that you receive
But on the gospels that you share
Not on your stability
But on your character
Not on the success that you earn
But the significance of the lives you change
A life that matters is a life that cares

Lots Of Time

There are 60 seconds in a minute
There are 60 minutes in an hour
There are 24 hours in a day
There are 7 days in a week
There are 4 weeks in a month
There are 12 months in a year
There are 10 years in a decade
There are 10 decades in a millennium
There is plenty of time
But the that has past is something you can't get back
So be wise with what you do in the time that passes you by

Mine

My pride belongs to me
My emotions belong to me
My dignity belongs to me
My talent, I train for
My knowledge, I study for
My wisdom, I embrace my experiences
What belongs to me is mine
Keep your hands to yourself
Keep your words to yourself
Stair if you must
Intimidate me you won't
But just remember this one thing
You can't take anything I don't give you

Mistakes

Everyone makes mistakes
I make mistakes
You make mistakes
It's in our nature as a human being to make mistakes
Mistakes can happen anywhere, in any way, and at any time
But how do you Handel those mistakes that you make
Do you mourn and dwell on them
Do you forget all about them
Do you use them to influence your future
I used dwell on mistakes I made
At times they left me thinking what if
And I thought that way for 20 years
I am beginning to realize things that were never really clear to me
People have forgiven me for mistakes I have made
And I find it hard to forgive people who have done me wrong
When in reality I have done worse, yet I was forgiven
I finally found the strength in my heart to forgive my dad
And I saw the talent in all the people I bullied
I saw the courage in all the people I beat up
And all the patience in those I mistreated
Everyone deserves to be forgiven of the mistakes that they make
I have always told myself this
But I could never bring myself to believe it
I refuse to allow myself to forget the mistakes I have made

And all the wrong that people have done to me
Because I can handle it
I am not going to dwell and let that anger build up no more
I will use it to influence my present and shape my future

Music

Music makes me feel a special kind of way
It's like a shape with many demissions
A pattern with a million designs
Like a book with an unlimited number of words
It fills my eyes with tears
It fills my heart with joy
It fills my muscles with movement
If fills my mind with intensity
It surrounds me
It speaks to me
It relaxes me
It knows me
It gets my every emotion
Music gets me through a typical day
Music turns my bad days to good days
Music just works so well with me
Music is just simply an important part of me

I Will See You Again My Friend

It was that sad sad day way back when
March 28, 1997
You left us and that was the day mom turned 30
If only you knew the things I would give
Just to be 1 year old again
Imagine what we could have done
Imagine what we could have been
I am proclaimed as the baby of the bunch
But you are the true baby brother of the 6
Would we even look alike
Would you be taller than me
Would we even have common interests
Stay up all night talking out our problems
Getting into silly brother fights
Causing trouble to our sisters as a hobby
Trying out for all the sports teams, me plus you
Stay safe my friend until we meet again
I promise to keep you in my heart till the very end
My little brother I will see you in a while

My Greatest Gift

My greatest gift is my ability to dream
I have always had a dream of want I want to be
Like the best football player to ever live
I dreamed of being a bug expert
But my dream had never really worked out
I came up in a struggle
My parents were separated
My little brother had passed away
I was bullied in school
I had turned into the definition of a troubled child
My dreams had become rattled
I came into high school a completely new person
I had the dream to become a winner
It was a tough road making lots of adjustments
Changing sports, diets, and friend groups
Even with all of the changes I only wanted to win
Until my race at Clayton my junior year of high school
I went into the race with a pretty bad injury
I got to the start line and I was in so much pain
But I still ran
So selfish, I only wanted to prove that I could beat someone
Even if I was injured
As we got deeper into the race I saw this kid
He was walking so I caught up to him
He said he wanted to PR but it was too hard
I told him I would help him, but had had to make me a promise
He promised me that he would not let me beat him

At the end of the race he finished with the time 28:54
His previous best was 34:46
After I crossed the finish line he greeted me
He hugged me and said
"Thanks I could not have done it without you"
At that very moment I realized
Winning isn't everything
And I found my greatest dream
I wanted to be a great leader
I wanted to be a great motivator
I wanted to be a great person
I feel God brought me up in a struggle for a reason
So that I could handle any situation
I will continue to dream of being great
As I feel that great things are destined to happen

My Race

As the sun shines
My face begins to glisten
Due to the sweat streaming from my face
Cameras everywhere
To record my miraculous finish
To snap shots of my memorizing face
To record the obnoxious sounds that I make
I pick people off one by one
The cluster starts to get thin
Until I am an outlier
So far ahead of the pack
But I am still running as hard as I can
Because I hear the roaring crowd
And I pass the line
With a new career best
And I throw my hands up, and I smile

My Time

This is my time
My time to shine
I thrive for improvement
I thrive for greatness
My desire is not for fame
My desire is for a better me
My life is nothing short of a blessing
Nothing short of a miracle
I just want to be remembered
Remembered as the guy who never gave up
I set my goals so high
So high that I fail to reach them
It gives my life meaning
I know my abilities
I know my flaws
I am destined to be somebody
That somebody is Dew Henson
I will be whatever I make of myself
And I plan to make myself the best I can be

Self-Respect

I know you think she is special
You see her with someone else
And it kills you mentally
But you can't dwell on it
You have to try to hide it
Because to you she may mean the world
But to her you may not mean anything
As hard as it is to accept
You have to find a way
It's not called being prideful
It's called having self-respect

Thanksgiving

Oh how I love to eat
My ham, my greens, and my delicious turkey meat
Although I love my food
That is not the meaning of the mood
It is a time to bond with the family at large
The love shows as if a negative charge
From the luck of the wish bone
To hiding those potent cell phones
With components from Black Friday Sales
And returning home with bellies the size of whales
How I love the sight of retreat
But I can't wait till our next meet

The Desk

Sweat off the hands of students rushing to class
Drool from student who stayed up all night
Gum from students who just don't care to be there
Crumbs from students who talked to much at lunch
Ugly art from students who don't care to pay attention
Farts that students let out in the middle of class
Books that were left because they were not needed
Homework left because of students not showing effort
Through all of this the desk still does what it is meant to do
Give the student a place to relax and learn

The Isle

It was time for a camping trip
Time to find a nice little lake to take a dip
I discovered a nice place on the northern isle
The floors were lined with a luxury golden tile
I booked the date in which I would stay
I even invited the gorgeous Lucy May
Unfortunately she declined my invite
She told me that it just didn't feel right
So I ventured to the isle by my lonesome
The drive there was consumed by boredom
But when I arrived my bags crashed against the ground
I stared blankly not making a single sound
I picked up my bags and retreated to my cabin
Upon my arrival I decided to go to sleep
as the sky began to blacken
I woke up to the birds singing their heavenly chime
There were no words, yet it sounded that of a rhyme
As the wind blew through the tall blades of grass
Popping out of the water I saw a high flying bass
I walked out to the field to admire the fresh new bloom
I sat down and analyzed this fascinating purple mushroom
I then proceeded to look up at the trees
And I witnessed the hard working honey bees
As they carried pollen back to their hive
I saw their population begin to thrive
I saw the turtles sitting upon the floating logs
I saw the moss the concealed the cute little frogs

I looked down at all the small schools of fish
They made the pattern of an abstract dish
I just looked at the crystal clear waters of the small lake
Even pinched myself to see if I was awake
Because it all seemed so unreal
The isle seemed to have the powers to heal
My overworked nerves had become calm
I held up my hand and just stared at my palm
Being on the isle filled me with happiness
But my departure had proven to fill me with sadness
I promised I would come back after a while
But at the time all I could do was smile

The Miracle Of Emerald

When a baby is born into the world to take its first breath
It is such a magical moment
Everyone wants to see and hold the baby
Emerald had that magical moment
However it was disastrous due to circumstances
She was a preemie coming 3 months early
She was diagnosed with RSV
Also known as Respiratory Syncytial Virus
Which is a highly contagious virus that infects the repertory tract
She was only given a 30% chance of life expectancy
Her size was very troubling
She weighed in at 2 pounds even
And measured in at 12 inches even
She has now been with us for over nine years
And she has grown tremendously
She was 2 pounds, she is now 107 pounds
She was 12 inches (1'); she is now 56 inches (4'8)
She was given a 30% chance to live, and a 70% chance not to
She defied all odds and she made it
My little cousin
She is like a headache waiting to happen
But her being with us is nothing short of a preemie miracle

The Strongest Person I Know

My mom is the strongest person I know
I look back at what I can interpret
And I just wonder
I cry, because I know I would have cracked
I play it off like I'm tough, but in reality I have a heart
And I do care about the feelings of others
But to have 6 kids with no effective father figure
4 girls with different dad's
To have your oldest daughter taken because you weren't ready
To have your son pass on your birthday
To lose your kids because you fell into depression
To go 3 years without seeing the son you had left
I was young I never really understood how bad it was
I had to grow up to understand it
I still remember how times I saw my mom
I also remember the amount of Times I talked to her on the phone
She and my sisters came down to see me one time
I only talked on the phone with her 12 times
The last phone call makes me mad at myself
My dad told her if she didn't get me that
day, she would never see me again
I hate myself for agreeing with something so terrible
Then I put my mom through several years of torture basically
And she never gave up on me
If it were me I would have given up
The amount of stress far exceeds what
any human should experience

And my mom is still behind me to this day
Through all my medical problems, she is there
I am blessed to have my mom in my corner
My mom is the toughest person I know
And she is my hero

Track

An activity at many
Throwing of a ball to a disk
Jumping for distance or height
Running for speed or distance
Perform in many locations
From a rubber track to a soggy sand pit
Wearing spikes or running shoes
It is a sport like very few
Everyone is allowed to wear running shorts
To the world know as short shorts
And men wear them to
They wear them and feel no shame
And many rise to fame
And sometimes get called lame
But it fails to be a game
It is a place to make your name
With athletes impossible to tame
With no two people exactly the same

Trap Door

It is not just a door
But a tunnel filled with gore
Many monsters dwell
Looking for a sweet sweet smell
Many fall into the dark
Where they are consumed like a shark
Even the strongest of the strong
Fail to leave with a pretty little song
People walk by in fear
Even shed the occasional tear
Walk by and take a glair
Better get ready to pull your hair
Because once you're hooked
Your stay will then be booked
For eternity you will rest
Everyday being put to the test

What You Taught Me

There are team sports and there are individual sports
But I love the sport of cross country
I especially love my cross country team
When I joined I was one of the best on the team
As I stayed with it I began to get better
But other people proved to be better than me
I often doubted myself
But I preached never giving up to my teammates
I hate when I hear people say I can't
But I often tell myself I can't or I won't
My team has taught me many lessons over my three year run
Mental preparation is more important that physical preparation
Performing in pain can be both good and bad
But most importantly
I learned there is no I in TEAM
I learned that if I let my feelings dictate how I run
Or I am not focused on the task at hand
I am not running for the team
I am being selfish
And therefore we can't win or fall as a team
And therefore I fall as an individual
They taught me that a team is not a team
Unless the team works as a whole
And is close like a family
We should have one pulse and one goal
That is how a team should operate
And that is what my family has taught me

What Is A Sport?

What is the purpose of sports?
Is it to win?
Is it to have bragging right?
Is it an excuse to be tired?
Is it motivation to try in school?
Is it to please your parents?
Is it your size?
What is it?
I know not everyone is an athlete out of sheer passion
Granted they are not for everyone
But they do accept many
A 450 man can play football
A 5'3 person can play basketball
A man with amputated legs can run in the Olympics
A girl can pitch in little league baseball
What's your excuse?

You Are Unique

Aside from our preferences we are not much different
We were both created the same way
Out of wedlock or not
Now our hobbies are different
Our personalities are different
Our features are different
But don't be a fool
Because your skin is no cleaner than my skin
No matter what comes in contact with it
No matter what it endures
You as an individual are no better than any other individual
Whether you be black or white
Short or tall
Fat or skinny
Smart or dumb
Lazy or athletic
Rich or poor
Homosexual, heterosexual, or even bisexual
These are all petty differences
That are often seen as overbearing differences
People are alike in many different ways
But our differences are what make us unique

You Can't Hold Me Down

So many times with my back against the wall
Constantly scared that it would allow me to fall
I can accept that I may be a liability
But I will always have a capability
So what if I have a burden on my back
I have a fire deep inside that is dying to attack
There are many abilities that I continue to lack
But the fact that I am even writing this now
You should stand up and give me a bow
Yeah I've been told "you can't" over and over again in my life
Yeah I've been told "you won't" over and over again in my life
So many times I have been told that I don't have what it takes
But look at what I've done
I have always been told that I only have one shot
And it is a shot I am always willing to take
Because I have nothing to lose
With myself being the only person that I have to prove
No matter the situation
No matter the state of mind
No matter the outcome
Whether it be negative
Whether it be positive
I don't care if I am a liability
But don't let that shape the way you view me
Because the way you view me is just an opinion
I am my own person
The only opinion that matters to me is my own

Now I may be forced to change my ways
But I will continue to advance in life
Because the world has an unlimited number of opportunities
And I have many skills
Athletics will forever be my passion
Now I won't always be an athlete
But that topic is yet to distort my mind
I will be ready when the time comes
Although a hobby isn't a passion
I still enjoy participating in my hobbies
So I will thrive no matter what in my life
And that is because I refuse to let myself give up and quit
That is the meaning of my mind
Because I am always following right behind
Causing many faces to express a frown
Because just simply they fail to hold me down

Your Name

I wrote your name on a piece of paper
But the wind blew it away
I wrote your name on my hand
But I washed it away
I carved your name into a tree
But the tree rotted away
I chiseled your name into a rock
But the rock crumbled away
I typed your name all over my computer
But it crashed and corrupted all of my data
I often bring your name up in conversation
But there is always someone to degrade you
It is hard to promote your name on simple things
So I found a place no one can touch it
I carved your name into my heart
And there it will forever remain

My Quest For You

Girls in the schools
Girls at the clubs
Girls in the streets
Girls are simply everywhere
But how do I find the one for me
It's like looking for a needle in a hay stack
I look to the left
I look to the right
I search high
I search low
I'll travel down every single road
I'll soar to the highest peaks in the mountains
I'll plunge to the darkest depths of the sea
Oh the things I would do
Just so that I can be with you
My quest has yet to come to an end
My expedition is getting rougher as I defend deeper
The heart break of not having you in my life
But I can wait for the day that we meet
Until then I will continue my quest for you

The Process

My life is not always been the desired type
It was hard for me in so many ways
I have health problems
I don't come from a wealthy family
I am not overly athletic or incredibly intelligent
I am a hard worker
And I have a ton of confidence in myself
However I hit a fork in the road as a senior in high school
I had my set on going to a university to run
I had it all planned I got my grades up
Abd worked hard at becoming a better runner
But epilepsy happened and derailed me
I went from know what I wanted to being lost
The Lord always had me though
Even when I was talking down on people
And making fun of others
I brought one of the greatest families into my life
I was invited to church and I didn't know what to expect
I was hoping that something good would come from going
To my surprise a lot of good happened
I became a Christian
I had so many doors open for me
And I made great new friends who will keep my head right
But I didn't know this would happen
I was poor in my soul
I had no hope
I am not a rich person I could not buy my way into college

So I had to find motivation to work hard at finding a different way
My desire and hunger for a better life less me
to Christ and he did not disappoint
He always has his eyes on you
No matter who you are

Author Biography

My name is Andrew Henson, but I like to be called Dew. I started writing poetry when I was a senior in high school. I took creative writing only because it was the most interesting class available at the time. I started out writing short stories, but I wasn't very fawned of them. I wrote a few poems and I liked writing them instantly. I like that they don't have to be very long, and I love that they don't have to be written in paragraphs. Writing became a way for me to release my anger without using words or physical contact. I have had it very tough my entire life, so I know what it's like to be down, and feel like you amount to nothing. I just want to be an inspiration or a role model to people who don't have one.

Made in the USA
Monee, IL
03 August 2020

37409520R00062